CUPPA COMFORT COLORING
COLOR ME SASSY
A Not-So-Motivational-But-Totally-Relatable
Coloring Book for Women Over 30

©2022 Michelle Baker Design LLC
All Rights Reserved
First Edition: November 2022

The designs in this volume are intended for personal use only and may be reproduced for that purpose only.

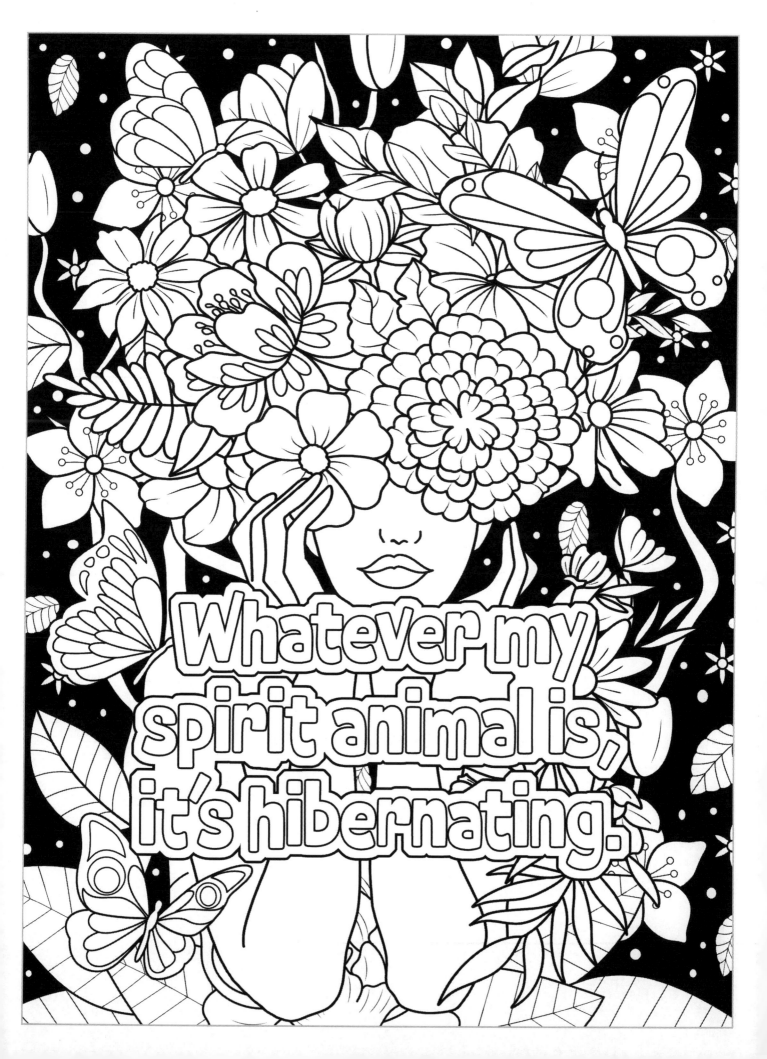

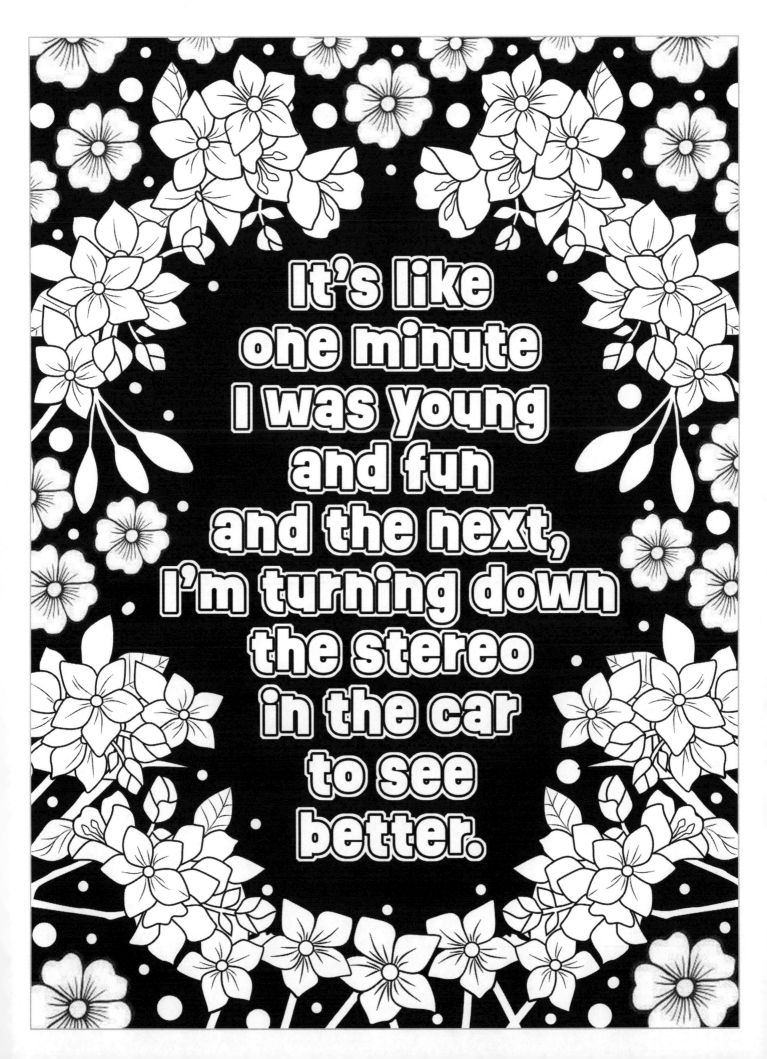

WE WANT TO SHOWCASE
YOUR BEAUTIFUL COLORING!
SHARE YOUR IMAGES TO INSTAGRAM
AND TAG:

@cuppacomfortcoloring

CUPPA COMFORT COLORING

©2022 Michelle Baker Design LLC
All Rights Reserved
First Edition: November 2022

The designs in this volume are intended for personal use only and may be reproduced for that purpose only.

Made in the USA
Columbia, SC
09 November 2022